Anything in Turquoise

To Vickie —

WENDY KLEIN

lots of love,

Wendy x

CinnamonPress

INDEPENDENT INNOVATIVE INTERNATIONAL

Published by Cinnamon Press, Meirion House, Glan yr afon, Tanygrisiau
Blaenau Ffestiniog, Gwynedd, LL41 3SU www.cinnamonpress.com
The right of Wendy Klein to be identified as author of this work has been asserted
by her in accordance with the Copyright, Designs and Patent Act, 1988. Copyright
© 2013 Wendy Klein ISBN: 978-1-907090-74-5. A CIP record for this book can be
obtained from the British Library.
Designed and typeset in Palatino by Cinnamon Press. Cover from original artwork
by Ray Hedger © Ray Hedger, 2012 from an original idea by Stephen and Wendy
Klein. Cover design by Jan Fortune Printed in Poland
Cinnamon Press is represented in the UK by Inpress Ltd www.inpressbooks.co.uk
and in Wales by the Welsh Books Council www.cllc.org.uk

Acknowledgments:

The poems in *Bubbe Meises* represent the contents of a pamphlet
submission which was short-listed in the Poetry Business
competition (2011), adjudicated by Carol Ann Duffy. Other poems
have appeared in competition anthologies, including *Snap,*
Templar pamphlet competition 2010, Battered Moon, 2012, Ware,
Ver, Virginia Warbey 2010 and 2011, and Norwich Writers 2011,
along with magazines and journals including *The Frogmore Papers,
Magma, Mslexia, Aesthetica, Artemis, The North* and *Smiths Knoll.*

Thanks are due to Martin Malone, poet and creative
writing facilitator, who combed through the draft manuscript
with a finely-honed razor, to Stephen Wilson who employed a
lighter touch, but was also helpful, and to all the members of my
workshops in Oxford, Swindon and Reading who have helped me
to iron out wrinkles, and most especially to my husband, Stephen,
my first port of call, who provides constant support and comfort
as and when needed. And last but not least, thanks to my editor
Jan Fortune, who made the miracle happen not once, but twice.

The quotations are used by kind permisssion of authors
and publishers: Bubbe Meises quote p.7 by Sasha Frieze, from her
blog:sashinka.blogspot.co.uk; epigraph by Edna St. Vincent Millay
(p.14) from *Selected Poems, The Centenary Edition,* (1992), Carcanet
Press; Chase Twichell epigraph (p.19) from 'The Condom Tree', in
Perdido (1991), Faber and Faber; Psalm 90:10 in epigraph p.25 from
King James Version Bible, Cambrige University Press; epigraph
from *Olive Kitteridge* by Elizabeth Strout (p.51), Simon & Schuster
UK Ltd, (2008).

Contents

Bubbe Meises

East

Elsewhere

Anything in Turquoise

Take this stone…share your vision, walk your talk…
Native American

Pairings

...ficus carica, one of the most ancient fruits
enjoyed in human history...

The perfect marriage is not between equals.
There must, said my grandmother -- be a sense
of savoury on sweet -- fibrous disturbance,
a tease of textures. Take the fig, winner
of the best-shaped fruit award, firm at first,
but dissolving to sweet pulp on the tongue,
blurred as yesterday, certain as tomorrow.

Pair it with a sliver of cheese, cheddar,
not brie, at best a seduction which may cloud
the palate. You can sink your teeth into this fruit;
its unashamed gape of readiness,
at the spot the gall wasp seeks to pollinate.

Now roll the gold-melt crumble inside your mouth;
your eyes close slowly and the earth may move.

Bubbe Meises

Bubbe Meises aren't really old wives' tales; they're the cloth you're wrapped in at birth, and the fabric of your shroud when you die.

Sasha Frieze

A Short Manhattan Lullaby, 1939

I see them tarting themselves up for the party where they'll meet;
she post-divorce from her approved-of Jewish ex,
and all set to become a successful playwright. I see her pucker up
for the brightest lipstick, slip her feet into lethal stilettos,
bat blackened eyelashes in the gilded mirror,
see it return her appreciative glance. He's more nervous;
primed with Dutch courage — Bourbon, because
he can't afford Scotch — tweaks a pre-formed bowtie,
covers a less-than-fresh shirt with a Harris tweed jacket –
herringbone. I see them arrive separately on the steps
of an East-Village Brownstone, pause a moment
before climbing the dim-lit stairs, gauging the level
of booziness, assessing the volume of laughter,
of music. He's the wrong man for her — literary, unreliable,
full of unattainable aspirations — the sort of stray she finds
irresistible. She's spiky, too smart for him,
but she's yet to find out. He can't resist her green eyes,
made brighter with kohl, alcohol, artifice, her sassy chat;
can't take his eyes off her carmine lips,
the flash of white teeth, bared by her brassy laugh,
and she can't resist his smoky gaze.
They go through the pick-up in cliché Technicolor,
and every warning she's heard about weak, irresponsible
gentile men wafts out the window of the ninth floor,
gains speed over the Hudson, the East,
as she whispers *shut up Mother,*
and I want to say *stop; you'll destroy each other,*
but I bite my tongue, just watch them walk away,
clinging to each other so tight that I flinch.

Spielerei

Wine helps to open the heart to reasoning, Rabbi Huna

Shikker, like stick her
or liquor:

what he called my father,
and my uncle Roy —

shikker shaygits,
drunken gentiles,

his sons-in-law
his girls' poor choices:

the one a *schlemiel,*
always bungling,

the other a *schlemazl,*
always bungled.

And he had to stand by,
keep *shtum*; watch them

the one a shlong,
the other a shmuck—

my grandpa,
his own daughters—

scheisse, shlepper,
shlump.

All that schlush-ing—
so Germanic…

By three things,
says the Talmud,

does a man
give himself away:

by his tumbler,
his tippling, his temper.

Screensaver, 1941

My mother looks down at her feet;
her high-heeled platform shoes,
her city-girl suit, so out of place

among her Connecticut in-laws,
relaxed in 'weekend casual'.
Her sister-in-law, twin to Brunhilde,

drapes a heavy arm around her neck,
while my goyish grandmother, not yet
away with the fairies, exudes radiance,

her own feet laced up in old-lady-posh.
Beside her, Auntie May sports careless
mix and match, idles with a cigarette;

narrows her eyes against smoke, sunlight
or the madness that will overtake her soon.
Cousin Patty is there, too — kitted out

in everyday-schoolgirl: saddle-oxfords,
bobbysox, thick glasses. It's their sturdy
comfy style horrifies my poor mother.

Digitised sepia picks out her tongue, its way
of protruding through lips too dark, too full;
the Semitic tongue she's sharpening for later,

when she'll lacerate the soulless goyem,
stamp them with labels: *the Amazon sculptress;
the fish-eyed schoolgirl; mishuganah May;*

lurching towards incarceration, divorce
death. My clever mother who barrelled
through her short life on irony and insults;

her eyes avoid the photographer, my father,
who held her future in his hands, let it slip
through his fingers. She might have stayed

to teach me what humour conceals,
about the anxious soul that lurks
in every stand-up comic: every Jew.

How my mother was born, 1906

*Childhood is the kingdom where nobody dies
nobody who matters that is.* Edna St. Vincent Millay

She hates to tell the story;
she loves to tell the story

but the story tells itself
by the haunted light

of the teardrop lamp.
I know it by heart:

how she gave birth at sixteen —
in a one-room tenement

with a fumbling midwife
and her husband excluded,

not before he got that old woman
to wash her filthy hands.

The searing pain and so much
blood: the birthing tool

that grazed the baby's face.
Every time she tells it,

her eyes, the green of lamp glass,
fill with tears as she remembers

her lengthy labour, her daughter's birth,
her premature death.

Even then, I knew how babies were born,
clenched my private muscles, shivered.

Button box

The silver ones have seen a lot of action,
decorated two cardigans, one for a boy; one
for a girl and a red knitted jacket for Penny.

So popular are they that a fight ensues
each time a garment dies, or is outgrown,
and they're free again, all four, faces bright as ever.

The brown leather ones are scuffed but still full
of themselves, certain of their immortality,
their future assured by two generations

of grandfathers and fathers who never notice
when they drop off in the office, on the train. They rise
to Grandma's touch at once when she lifts the lid,

exclaims, *Aha, I knew you were there.*

But it's the tiny white ones that keep the world together,
pearly shells with two or four holes;
they huddle in handfuls, clatter when disturbed,

and though they look identical, they're tricksy, titter
amongst themselves, with their secret knowledge
of how they're always and always not quite the right size,

at our stupidity in believing all whites are the same.

Needlepoint

She's watching the new Sunday series.
She doesn't know what it's called yet,
and she'll probably forget to watch it next week,
unless I remind her —
if I'm here to remind her —
if I can bear to be here to remind her.

Anyway, she's not really watching;
she's doing her special needlepoint –
not like those printed pictures you buy
in boutiquey sewing shops —
the ones that tell you every colour you should use.

She just keeps a roll of canvas behind the sofa
along with a patchwork bag of yarn;
cuts off a length, grabs
a handful of colours,
frowns them into submission, starts.

In the cathode flicker of the constant screen,
tapestries emerge of owls and flowers,
of land and seascapes,
an impressionist universe
in her bedroom.

She hands me a piece of stiff canvas
watches as I take it in my hands,
breathe in its rough new-cloth smell,
smiles encouragement, offers
me her wool, balls of all sizes,
neatly wound, one after the other,
night after night in front of her TV.

I take some black yarn,
moisten it with my tongue, jam it
into the thick tapestry needle
while on the screen, Fred Astaire
begins to dance on the ceiling.

Menagerie

If I find my way it is via sage, rubbing it between my fingers,
testing its fragrance, musty and sharp under my nose,

and I am where my grandmother is cutting up chicken for soup.
I am three, four, maybe five, huddled in a rush-bottomed chair,

cradling my stuffed horse, nose pressed against his cropped
cotton-string mane; the points of his felt ears, cruelly scissored off

by a naughty neighbour, are intact again. His embroidered eyes
gaze up at me, still full of quiet suffering, though in the photo,

it is my eyes that are brimming, my mouth turned down.
If I find my way back, the stuffed cat will be there too, grey

with a white bib, looking more like its living counterparts:
glass eyes that pierced my own. How I was haunted and alarmed

at their eternal wide-openness, and there's the stuffed fawn
I knew was Bambi, but it is the fourth animal that troubles me;

whether it was lost or whether it ever existed. I shuffle the black
and white photos of myself at three, at four, at five,

when they sent me back.

The Puberty Tree

...sex makes lost things reappear... Chase Twitchell

Tree? There was always a tree. Sometimes it was pine –
all needles and soughing – dallying

with any breeze that came along, or maybe copper beech,
its roots busy undermining our foundations.

If I go back to thirteen, it was Jacaranda erupting
in puffs of purple smoke, or Eucalyptus,

dropping brutal gum nuts on the dahlias. My grandmother
is there, young enough to laugh

without crying; her hands stained red with pomegranate juice
or henna, or some new colour

she has chosen to paint her world happy again, bring back
my mother, her dead daughter; the memory as raw

as sunrise or sex.

Four Black Teas

One for my aunt, the only real tea drinker in the family, and a bleak noxious substance it was, black as insomniac nights — her lipstick on the morning mug, the afternoon bone china. If she had a box called caddy, I don't remember it, or whether it was just a cardboard replica like the self she kept separate, sipping through the day, the night, her short life, instead of eating.

One for my stepmother — out of season and I didn't want to be there long after we'd outgrown family holidays — but she needed her medicinal cup of tea, the kind she only drank when she was, she thought, coming down with something. I remember how the old waitress shuffled in, rubbing sleep from her eyes, the smell of unwashed body that hovered around her like gnats.

One for my sister-in-law who brought me a cup that morning in 1968, as if she were a magus bearing priceless substances to the infant Jesus, the bright mug that shrieked Hallelujah, and the infant growing inside me, who lurched with revulsion before she turned her back.

One for my kids — me on my own with them again, when someone kicked someone under the table — it never takes longer than a few minutes at tea-time, for everyone to revert to the state of nature, like a party marooned by a shipwreck: the fish fingers slightly charred, their father absent, the youngest who noted matter-of-factly: *mummy you look like you need a hug*. How I took it.

Coffee with Rae

My grandmother's got her chance at last to advise
Miss Taylor, Mrs. Hilton, Mrs. Wilding, Mrs. Fisher,
Mrs. Todd, Mrs. Burton (twice,) and the rest, but not yet —
on her wardrobe, her morals (her conversion!), her career.

Right there in the Rachel-pristine kitchen of my childhood,
she settles her favourite star into Grandpa's cane-bottomed
chair, the famed buttocks succulent, a snug fit; the perfect
breasts pressed against the round whiteness of the kitchen table
as one set of famous eyes locks with another.

Now if you want my advice, Liz (of course she does,
that's why she's here, but Rae is being polite today),
May I call you Liz? You call me Rae — and she leaves
no time to risk a reply — *you'll need*, she continues,
*to stop this carry on, treat yourself to some clothes that fit,
cut back on the false eyelashes and wait for a role
that stretches you* — *maybe Shakespeare*, she breathes,
and winks at the lady in red, as she lifts her coffee cup
to salute the occasion, while Liz looks on in awe
because no one drinks coffee like Rae, the cup
overflowing, the saucer sloshing.

Now about that Tennessee Williams, Liz, she goes on,
and the star of *Cat on a Hot Tin Roof,* looks abashed, shields
her five-star cleavage with fluttering fingertips. *You'll get further,
maedele, if you don't bare all believe me, that's something I know,*
says Rae, as she plonks down her cup with a murky splash
and a far-away look, while the actress waits, her violet gaze
expectant as the mantle clock strikes a strident three,

and they get right down to it in the crazy California afternoon.

The Necktie Quilt

After his death at eighty three, which she believed
was premature and the fault of paramedics
who'd 'taken their time' to arrive,

she set about thirty years of his neckties, the gifts of grateful
clients whose grubby affairs he'd settled in and out
of court, while she'd looked on,

applauding his victories, folding away ties. Now she selected only
the silk ones, unpicked them with meticulous
care, pressed them under a damp cloth

until every crease was smoothed, arranged them on the table
in the dining room: the bold paisleys, their backs
curled against regimental stripes,

the gaudy florals, which had made him smile, but were never
worn, cheeky polka dots, a couple of sombre knits
she suspected were synthetic.

Day after day, the old Singer hummed and whirred as she stitched
the strips together, and when the backing was attached,
the borders feather-stitched by hand;

she found a place for every scrap left over: trim for a dresser scarf
appliqué for scatter cushions, a white curtain tied back
with a sash of hand-painted peacocks,

an old dressing gown with a new belt, flaunting wild geometrics.
Swathes of unexpected colour cropped up
in unexpected places,

the fallen-fruit silks of mulberry, gold and plum, a splash
of scarlet in an inner sleeve, reminding her
of the flash of a whore's petticoat —

a certain woman she saw once, slipping out of his office.
When it was finished, she shook it out,
flung it across her single bed.

Just Jacaranda

The colour makes you gasp,
and knowing you can't describe it; that words
are too usual: that bloody *purest blossom blue* —
the best Steve Tilston could manage —
or maybe just admit it makes you hyperventilate;
or consider the concept of ocular orgasm,
coarse, but compelling, or think of the Hebrew: *tehelet*,
the silk thread woven into your grandfather's unused
prayer shawl, though in Buenos Aires the locals claim
it's able to whistle Tango tunes on demand,
and when you see it dressed up in its Christmas skirts,
pirouetting down the streets of Adelaide to Tchaikovsky
in unimaginable, unutterable, brazen, dauntless blue,
you stop trying to give it a name, remember the way
that naming implies possession — birth to death —
and you, above all, across continents and seas
where snow bends branches until they weep and snap,
cannot possess it; but only the link you make
to your childhood when you first saw its glory, before
blossom carpeted the ground, before you were left
with green silence, tracery of fern, naked foliage;
like the time your grandfather or someone said,
it blooms in places where old Jews go to die.

My Grandfather Quotes Psalm 90

The days of our years are threescore years and ten;
and if by reason of strength they be fourscore years,
yet is their strength labour and sorrow;
for it is soon cut off, and we fly away.

This is not the year to cut loose,
though loosening seems inevitable,
and losing, the terror of another decade
hurtling past, and I hear his voice;

I'd know it anywhere, ranting
about his own three-score and ten
in Old Testament sonority,
when he didn't believe a word of it,

declaiming in his best court-room style,
what he never believed in — I guess it was never,
though the Yeshiva boy he once was,
still crops up in my mind — that tiny portrait,

my memory-miniature, so small I keep it
tucked in my most secret pocket — the boy
who decided early he did not believe in G-d,
turned into the man who knew beyond doubt,

Psalm 90 was his personal prophecy,
began at once to begin the end; a task
which took him thirteen years to complete,
left me to seek a different prophet.

Marble

And there is her sigh, a noise that comes from a ghetto
somewhere east of Prague — a whoosh of breath that plays
out on a moan of protest — protest against the marble floor
that freezes her knees, its widening cracks that are never
proper-clean though she scrubs until her knuckles split;

and he just in the kitchen, at his post by the fruit bowl,
ear tight against the Bakelite radio, his hand that selects
a perfect navel orange, peels it in one continuous spiral,
its skin curled and fragrant against the table laid for later,
while the news drowns out her lament,

and the fight rages on in the steam, the weapon, ammonia,
the only substance known to *proper-clean*. Then it comes:
the crunch and squish of a bulky something, landing hard
on wood, a sound so urgent, Cronkite's voice expires
mid-prophecy, mid evening news,

and when I open the door after the last mourner leaves,
the room smells of pink: Cameo soap, thick shag rug,
clean-in-a-flash linoleum, no sign of grey marble,
ripped out after his last fall; her triumph of comfort
over the ten ammonia-free years without him.

The Death of Grandma Rae

Ignorant in the sense
that she left school at eleven
went to work in a shirtwaist factory
married at fifteen; a round girl,
a sturdy woman, not five feet tall
with full breasts, a once-tiny waist,
who never let him, a self-made man —
immigrant to big-shot lawyer —
get the better of her, in the sense
that if he shamed her in public,
she reminded him and the world
she'd taught him the parts of speech,
then cursed him on her deathbed
for all the years he'd held her back.

California Day

i.m. LHT, May 1942

It's typical L.A. just how you fell in love with it —
a lifetime away from snow and slush, remembered
brownstones. The house is a single-storey sprawl:

ranch-style Spanish with reliable roof tiles in red.
There's no place for fear in this balmy afternoon —
Gracie has sung the praises of the doctor,

and you giggle with your sister, plan chocolate sodas
for after, remind her, remind yourself, of the hundred and one
good reasons not to have it: the first one still so young,

the war still on, no money, no jobs. You've been told
it's a simple procedure, over in no time, but you're scared
of the pain, insist on ether. I imagine you poised

between thirty and forty, the high board of your life;
your arms pressed to your sides, waiting to black out
and when they tell me years later, I try to picture

the second before you made the dive; to guess
whether you spared a thought to who'd comfort
your sister who drove you there and waited;

or your parents miles away, not knowing,
and who would hold your first-born,
if you failed to surface again.

East

...and the old jeweller said,
'we in India are content with our world;
you rush around, but you are not content...'

I Greet the Blue Water Buffalo of Cambodia

O you are blue, not the casual blue of everyday sky,
the shade a child crayons in above a house
with a chimney and windows for eyes,
not even lapis lazuli, too decorative,
but blue enough to drown in.

O you are so blue, not the faded blue of denim jeans,
run up in a rush by a girl too young to work,
nor the periwinkle blue of tucked-away
blossoms in lands you'll never see
where your yoked presence is not
known or even dreamed of.

O your blueness is so much deeper than powder blue,
though far short of midnight, closer to sapphire,
cornflower, steel. Yes, steel blue is the sheen
of your flanks, smoothed over muscles that
undulate in time to your master's demands
as you plough his rice paddies to feed
his family, the world.

O bend down your smiling horns so I can touch your great
blue head: ruffle the silk fringe that springs up on top,
admire those horizontal ears, stretched wide, as if
eager to hear, to understand.

The Pavements of Ulaan Bataar

They are set skewed, a craze of cracks
like weathered maps,

their edges fraying into some strong-
smelling herb that might be

camomile, sprawled near grass so sparse
as to be overlooked

or turned feral, its blades cheeky,
blatant in their thrust

into concrete, into tarmac. Beggars
skulk, sidle up with toddlers

who mumble stale buns through tear-
stains, clutch plastic bottles

of milk diluted grey, watch their mothers' lips
form their sole English word — *hungry,*

hungry. Young girls caper there, too,
in gaggles, in short skirts, sin-tight,

tapping to the click and chink of stilettos
strapped to dainty ankles — lean-

line legs that go on forever, promise
nothing beyond their gift of beauty.

They text on cell phones, broadcast
messages from snug t-shirts that strain

to cover mannequin breasts: *'deep-laid joke'*,
'Marilyn Manson', *'Eco-smile'*,

'Don't waste my time', and finally,
'Expectation, reason's whore', here –

where she clings — round all our necks,
reminds us how far we are from home.

The Natural History of Ulaan Bataar

Having stepped from the gabble of the street
onto buckling lino
that crackles underfoot

Having shut my nostrils to the reek of bleach
that saddens the corridors
of this government museum

Having fled past the room of the astronauts,
Mongolian and Russian, blazing
with shared Soviet pride, braved

the woolly rhino's faded photo, his bones
spread out on a counter painted
hopeful meadow green,

met the chinless gaze of the Arctic hare, her doubt-
filled eyes, cotton wool snow tucked
on a branch behind her head

Having flinched before the snarling Siberian wolf,
futile and moth-eaten behind glass,
her stuffed cubs at her feet

Having opened myself to Shamanic legend —
the duty of the wolf to bring nurturing,
wildness, wolf-ness into the world

Having failed and failed to grasp lessons
about cultures in varying states of disrepair;
having walked away even sadder.

Dressing the Dearest Child

It is an ancient Mongolian tradition to dress the 'dearest' (or dangerously ill)
child in special clothing in the belief that the dress will serve as protection…

A young girl, her nose pressed against the museum glass,
yearns toward the display of costumes sewn for the dearest child:
her dress of protection, the orange of Mandarins for sun-warmth
to keep her alive a little longer. Nearby, her mother sees
how she covets the garment, its flowers stitched in sapphire,
colour of calm, the splashes of poppy, the peplum spangled
with Genghis gold, shoulders padded, ready to receive the wings
that will carry her to safety when her time on earth runs out.
The mother watches her, leaning in, moves closer, tugs hard
at her hand, tugs her back from what she cannot grasp, the death
awaiting the dearest child, her brightly-coloured shroud.

The Little Brown Elephant

*In 1912 the Bogd Khan, last religious emperor of Mongolia, purchased for
22,000 roubles, a little brown elephant, who was transported for 8 months,
by train and foot, to Ulaan Bataar.*

Fresh blossoms would have greeted
the little brown elephant: incense, a plated
crown draped with red velvet, fringes
of coral and pearl tickling his papery ears.

Between the three lamas hired to care for him;
he would have walked, trunk swaying in time
to his easy gait, the drone of the *morin khur*,
unaware of what awaited him: the whip crack

to teach him circus tricks, the chain that would
tie him in front of the winter palace, his slow
starvation, forgotten after the death of his master,
the triumph of the people. Today men scatter

grass seed on dry flower beds, hope for rain
to green it; trundle home with back-ache, loaded
with beer and vodka, to rooms in concrete blocks
to drink and dream open meadows, wild horses.

Portering

The legs of the porters
    stem from the slenderest branches
        of the tallest trees,
                the eldest carry the heaviest bags, always

They spring from a matted undergrowth
    of wiry, venous material
        that starts as sepia, weathers to bronze
                their arms hang relaxed at their sides
                to provide balance

Their roots may vie for living space
    but their colours
        are all the shades of earth

                they make nests of cloth
                    to support their load;
                their faces are almost expressionless.

The Gobi Looks on

She glimpses sheep dispatched in a flash,
　　no blood spilled,
　　　　just a quick squeeze to the heart
　　　　　　eyes dulled,
　　　　　　　　and quiet.

She eschews waste-bins;
　　her waste is not secret: the skeleton of a camel
　　　　its head more or less intact, the single
　　　　　　shin-bone of a gazelle, its hoof
　　　　　　　　sand-polished through summer,
　　　　　　　　　　perfected by winter.

She monitors the clouds that cluster
　　round her edges like curds in whey,
　　　　circling the bowl-brim
　　　　　　of her particular sky;
　　　　　　　　becomes an avid collector of tyres,
　　　　　　　　　　their husks that sprawl, mangled by her heat.

She meditates on the Ibex, clocking his time,
　　his horn rings that notch up the years
　　　　until his head becomes too heavy;
　　　　　　when she points the way to the high-enough cliff
　　　　　　　　where he'll stand till his weight topples him.

She oversees her necessary scavenger —
　　the sated buzzard, too heavy to fly,
　　　　who seeks a rock-face, and like a glider,
　　　　　　finds the thermal lift.

She protects the thigh-bone of an eighteen-year old girl,
　　decorated with the blue of heaven,
　　　　the yellow of the sun, oversees its sacred use.

She watches over Nomads,
　　in the damp-felt whiff of their tent-homes after rain,
　　　　she dries everything out with her hot breath; stands by
　　　　as the women milk their mares — listens
　　　　　　for their whispered word for wild horse —
　　　　　　　takhi — its tone of reverence

The Sand Sweeper of Kovalam

She will not be eclipsed by the bedspread man
who plays at statue-making; poses against
a seascape, a few palms for effect, his wares
perched on his head, fanned out in a pyramid
of rainbow pleats as he tempts passers-by
with swirls of fabric. She just sweeps on,
decked out in the violent chaos of colour
of roadside gardens where sudden poinsettias,
waggle their thick crimson tongues, spread
their flames against tea plantations, green
as as my grandmother's eyes. I try to imagine
the sand sweeper at night where the rarer
yellow-golds join in, cackle at their scandal,
but I lose my bearings: what she does
in her spare time, where she goes.

Old Woman Riding High

How they watch me ride, hunched
and sweating on my fat gel saddle,
mysterious under my space-man helmet:
through malodorous villages, past
fruit-sellers who are astonished
at my speed, past prune-faced old men,
who adjust their mundus in alarm, check
the lay of their testicles, spit.

How the children cheer or mock me,
this pale-faced grandmother with gears,
who fails to understand their words
which might be ridicule or wonder
at a new approach to mad old women;
let them burn themselves out,
but the pineapple woman wonders
what's the hurry. She has carried

a pineapple on her head for three days,
re-tracing the same route, undaunted
by our lack of interest, her produce
a Carmen Miranda fruit bowl hat.
I guess it might be the same pineapple
that she takes home at nightfall, places
on her meagre table, ordinary as breakfast rice,
ready to set on her head the next day,

like a crown or a halo. As it ripens
its value may increase; there is always time,
as that Keralan grandmother riding side-saddle
on a Royal Enfield knows. Sari a billow
of colours, she gazes back at my last great hill;
regal and wise, raises her hand as if in blessing,
though her eyes seem to say, if I want to save time
I should find a man with a motorbike.

Kovalam to Trivandrum

I'm alone as I step over the sleeping bodies;
the woman in her crumpled sari,
her baby curled next to her tousled head.

I'm not the child in a red-belted coat
with matching beret; carsick
each time on the way,

or even her older self, the woman
in the Jackie K. pillbox hat, half-veiled,
her fox fur collar turned up high,

and this is not the Carquinez Bridge,
though the struts are as rickety
over the churning Meenachil.

I've avoided the rubbish piled
everywhere and that sleek black cow,
content to nibble a cardboard box.

Here I am at a junction where
Alec Guinness plays Indian
for David Lean,

and this time I don't have to mind the gap,
be nuzzled by the whiskery aunties,
don't have to gag

on peanut butter sandwiches, bleeding
grape jelly. I can scoop *chana masala*
with *paratha*, using my right hand only,

suck my fingers, savour the dust and grime,
the satisfying greyness of the platforms
through streaked windows, where passengers

are hunched like boulders draped in bright cloth,
where businessmen hold their briefcases aloft,
adjust their lunghis to avoid the chocolate puddles.

The chambermaid will marvel at the relics
I've left behind, empty tubes of cream and paste,
metal and plastic. Down the track

the light is green — not like emeralds
or grass — but haunted like jade,
and it's urging me to go, go, go.

In praise of the children who sell scarves at Angkor Wat

They celebrate the divinity of free enterprise,
for though they travel in flocks, each,
like a homing pigeon, represents himself.

Their teeth are white and razor-sharp,
the better to bleed us dry
of compassion and currency,

but their arms are filled with rainbows. They coo
and croon their wares, *you buy my scarf —
one dollar?* They do not accept *no,*

or understand it, and sated with scarves
we are each, in turn, satisfied with the deal.
They honour us

with their attention, *you come back soon?*
And we shower them with bills,
grateful for their beauty.

A Boat People

Hardly a surprise that they took to the water, these river folk with
their floating markets, their floating villages.

Hardly a surprise that picking up the oars of ramshackle crafts
could seem like a solution when six year old children

can row their younger siblings, standing up, gliding forwards,
the logic of it, compared to our Western style —

travelling with our backs turned towards where we are going.
Here in the Mekong, they row to the middle where tour boats

glide among the water hyacinths. They wave tiny bananas
like bright yellow fingers, a fruit of unimaginable sweetness —

point with pride to the family pineapples stacked in the stern,
show us how they are the ripest and best. Painted on the bows,

the eyes of their boats are fixed on us as they approach —
eyes wide open, to show them where they are going.

Remnants

Like some space-age insect, the American helicopter,
blades throttled by time and midday heat, hunches
just inside the gate of the War Remnants Museum,
beached forever, where I too, am caught and pinned,

my throat closed by emotion, pollution, or both, choked
by the memory of a million late-night newsreels — the television
images of my father's nightmares. Saigon is falling all around me,
a stampede of urgency unimaginable in this sleepy afternoon

in Ho Chi Minh City. Hawk-eye Pearce crouch-runs across
my memory to tend incoming wounded. Jimi Hendrix
twangs his tormented *Star Spangled Banner* while I touch
a B-52 bomber, grounded alongside tanks, now harmless toys.

Two grey-haired businessmen in their sixties share a bench
in the shade; the hands of one the right age for rolling joints,
the other for hacking out tunnels. At rest, yet restless,
they punch out emails on their iPhones, texting ghosts.

Border

Behind me Vietnam
where Piranhas
make a bomb crater
their home
feed a village,
a tourist industry,
where girls
in long white gloves
ride mopeds
their hair
jet waterfalls
where a woman pinched
my husband's arm,
whispered
goodbye

Before me
the Tower of Skulls
where the twenty thousand
are stacked in rows
and I see a girl
head bowed
fingering a single rosebud
and back away
full of respect
to see she's talking
on her mobile phone

Cambodia Sunday

Naked babies
brown and shiny
to match the mud
squirm at being scrubbed
slip through the hands
of surprised grannies
who laugh and scold
as grannies do

The glide and flow
of monks
their shaven-heads gleaming
dome-like in smoggy sun
the flutter of saffron robes

the plod and splash
of skinny white cattle
where stick figure men
push ploughs up and down rice rows
all the shades of emerald and jade

Houses spindly on stilts
that look too fragile to support them
lean in
over murky pools
where scratchy fowl
dispute over water rights

truckloads of masked workers
ride jammed in tight
their eyes inflamed
by dust and fumes
from mopeds from buses

Pagodas spring up in fields
their stacked tiers
arms held out in prayer
supplicants braced for regret
faces turned up to praise Buddha
or embrace another karma

Ox carts creak with age
and constant use
a landmine museum
displays a sign
Open to Visitors.

Tuol Sleng

The words in Khmer mean
'poisonous mountains'
and this place locks me out,

though my high school was a jungle —
knife-carrying girls, boys
who dreamed brass knuckles.

In this prison, once a high school,
ghosts inhabit classrooms
once turned into cells;

sprawl on naked bedsprings
that would have held mattresses
of kapok, soaked in urine and blood.

Black and white photos chart their history,
a single framed image for each imminent
death, galleries of portraits

in the rooms next door; startled faces,
dishevelled hair, clothing in disarray —
faces of all ages, captured

by the camera. My high school jungle
pales by comparison; tigers like tabby cats,
my tormenters, truculent toddlers.

Elsewhere

dying   not dying
either way
it tires you out

Elizabeth Stroud, *Olive Kitteridge*

Lagniappe

after Eudora Welty

She lands on a wedding cake,
where the wings of the plane flap,
fold, shudder with tenderness;
melt from the heat of a thousand

candles. She threads a path
through carnival where beauty
and vice stand, hospitably close —
fan themselves in doorways

under palmettos by day, lighted torches
by night. A flower opens. She feels
the pull of the bayou, and on her cheek,
the urgent rasp of Spanish moss that beards

the wetland Cypresses; sees he has strewn
her bed with Mardi Gras beads, the sparkle
of a thousand stones, a lagniappe to tempt her:
a little more for a little less before pay-time.

She lies down among fake gems that spike
the hollow between her shoulder blades,
imprint themselves — listens
for the vodun drums — for his step.

A lagniappe is from Southern Louisiana & Mississippi . Pronounced 'lan yap', it is an extra or unexpected gift or benefit presented by a store owner to a customer with the customer's purchase or as a tip for a waiter, porter, etc; also a regular custom during Carnival.

Patchworking

Mending her quilt
is a conversation
about ancestors,
not always her own —
about hands
that have come to the rescue,
threading a tactful needle-path
up and down calico rows
where pink centres make
a cheeky nod to polka dots
while a bold stripe takes up
a floral challenge —
is taunted by geometrics
or a sudden shift in theme.

I'm mending her quilt
a gaudy Katrina survivor,
its appliquéd squares
of cotton, of linen,
wearing out, wearing through
the seams slipping,
their stitches parting
from the near-transparent
fabric of old dresses
stitched into a web
of former lives, worn
tenderly by frugal women
then consigned
to generational ragbags —
the lost art of mending
the unmendable.

Potter's Field, New Orleans-Style

We owe respect to the living, to the dead
we owe only truth. Voltaire

Peeling paint, tilted headstones and bones
left by Katrina — vertebrae, fingers,
jaw fragments in the dirt, but we could
say they know how to bury their dead.

Black-crayoned letters spell out —
we miss you Mama, and next-door
The Jackson family, with a ragged list
of names and dates, added as needed.

A baby lies nearby under a battered pram,
a pink rattle hanging from the hood,
while someone's son provides his mother
with a deck chair, surrounds her plot

with a picket fence. Here in Holt the dead
live on, cosseted by the care of the living
who hold umbrellas up to shield them
from rain, picnic above them on Sundays,

allow children to run free over their heads,
bring paint to freshen faded lettering
or drawings, knowing for certain
that the best graffiti is new and true.

The woman who sold her garage
to buy a horse

She wakes up to the superiority of hay,
its fragrance rain-damp, sun-dry:
the scratch of straw, of warm breath
on cheek, of apples and sugar lumps
sucked from her fingers, savoured
with strokes of a lavish pink tongue,
the rust-proof finish of warm skin,
wild mane, tamed to curry-combed gloss.

The woman who sold her garage to buy a horse
finds out her palms are shaped for the slip
and pull of reins, ready to swap the swank
of upholstery, alloy wheels, for the toughened
calluses of pitchfork, stable-broom,
for the creak and clank of saddle and bit.

She turns her back on oil-slicked cement
revels in boots mired in manure:
finds her stride is longer; thighs braced
to rise to the trot; tosses her head
like some atavistic centaur, so tall
in the saddle, the clatter of hooves
below could be her own.

Narrowboat Wife

A narrow boat, he said, rolling the 'r's, making it sound
even narrower, and I, in my naïveté, conjured a romantic idyll,
agreed to look at photos. The flower pots and watering cans,

old-fashioned, hand-painted, brimming with Petunias, marigolds
ivy-leaf geraniums, worked on my good sense, though I know
I should have been suspicious with his babble of a past

in black and white, a future in colour. The clatter of the deck
under his feet, and suddenly he was all poet and dreamer, full
of the river's moods, the rain, the wind, the colour of the sky;

how first thing in the morning, your hands frozen (not that he
had ever rowed), *the sun just starting to creep to the eye line,
the river that feels like it's sleeping and you almost try not*

to wake it up... he marvelled, *like an iceberg, nine-tenths
of what you can see is below the water line.* Night after night
in my punishing bunk, I remember his words as I listen

for the plop of water voles, picture their dives to deep burrows,
futile against the sharp-toothed, greedy mink. I wake
to gang wars between cygnets, and worse, to surprise each day

at the ordinariness of it all: couch the same green velour
as the one in the cottage with its cushions of buttoned kapok,
same pine panelling, cheerful cups on hooks — more cramped,

but still in need of dusting — the ordinariness of retirement made
scarcely different by the river; its occupations, like marriage,
all to do with rescue and maintenance: swans, voles, pollution.

Dry shade

A problematical bed to fill was how she put it, which left a lot of scope to wonder how the problem came about and when. In her faded Greenham Common t-shirt and cut-offs, she looked too jaunty for sudden widowhood; too down-at-heel to be on the pull, though her breasts were nicely presented. She didn't seem the sort to offer her bed to a canine companion, and I guessed her to be a cat-hater or even a member of 'Abstinence Actually'. *Dry shade* she whispered to the young attendant, and the ghost of Mellors seemed to hover at her shoulder, to hint at maidenhair ferns, though a gamekeeper was probably the last thing she wanted in her garden, dry shade or not. Then she disappeared down a row of euphorbias, left me to conjure her maverick world; the delicate stepping over of a wine-and-poem-drunk woman, her late night dance, how in the morning she might hurry to 'sent items' to check her indiscretions.

A Short History of my Aversion to Libraries

Because they've put my life at risk,
and I'm only allowed when it's Daddy's Saturday.

I'm five, braced in the rumble seat of his '29 Desoto,
seat belts, decades away, books on my lap;

one of them finger-marked with breakfast butter.
Will there be trouble?

Because the open door makes my tummy ache;
the smell of polish and yellow paper — book breath,

the lady at the desk fierce behind her glasses,
though she smiles at my Saturday Daddy, pretends

not to notice my butter prints. Because you can die
in libraries, or get killed — so many books about it,

their covers bright with blood; body after body,
face down on the long, long tables:

a knife stuck in the back of one, bullet holes in another.
When I get a ticket for the Bodleian,

I'm afraid to use it; the book I'm looking for
is bound to be the one that's missing.

Re-painting the Cave with Jackson

unformed figure, Jackson Pollock, 1953

When he returned with his learning,
full of bombast and new ideas,
his travel sacks bulging with bright tins
that sprayed thick liquid, which,
     eyes shifty with mischief,
he would demonstrate to anyone prepared to watch,
     while declaring how bored he was
with the clumsy stick figures of cattle,
the sketchy outlines of people, scratched in
all that long time ago and fading, the walls yellowed
with smoke from our fires, blotched with the smudges
of naughty-fingered children, the angry stains
of badly-cooked food thrown by angry men and boys,
     we began, cautiously at first, to listen.

He revealed the instability of our reds,
our yellows, tossed out the iron ore we'd used to mix them,
our well-worn pestles and mortars, warmed by skilled
and loving hands, while mocking our charcoal blacks,
our crumbling-chalk whites.
     The women shuffled and muttered,
about his bizarre contraptions that could spray
the highest ceiling without the need to puff dizzily
into bird-bone blowpipes,
     but the younger ones listened to his rant,
fingered his stiff new brushes, rubbed them on their cheeks,
     their bare chests,
          relished the prickly tufts.

They made us go elsewhere while they peeled
and scrubbed away the old shapes, the lean-haunched
gazelles, bristling with arrows, the hunters bent to their bows,
our short-legged, hammock-bellied horses,
        but rumours drifted up to us on the hill
            where we'd been sent to wait:
        of terracotta bodies, bare and writhing, in a colour
richer than the rusty brown of wild plum root, and
        slashed through with yellows — a chromium that dulled
the old dyes of broom, lichen gold — and of deeper greens,
        not found on trees or hillsides.

        Invited to view his masterpiece, we stood, blinded
by this orgy of naked colour, already pining for our past.

I Borrow Aunt Ruby's *Jane Eyre*

Its olive greenness is already haunted, the spine
stiff with importance, lettered in gold

with wood engravings. I am barely twelve
when I open it, and the crocodile queue of girls

shuffles towards me off the cover, their starved faces
cut-out hearts and triangles, chins sharp enough

to slice bread. Their centre-partings are razor-ruled
in white, stretch from taut scalps. I gaze for hours

into the eyes of the only queue-waif who's dared
to look up, my sister in literature, sent away

after her mother's early death, to the bleakness
of boarding school, by an aunt who despises her.

I gorge on the gothic horror, the fodder of nightmares
that advances, gargoyle-faced as I turn each page:

the downcast eyes, the meagre capes, the cobblestone-
chill that seeps into boots unmended or too thin.

Flushed with deprivation or consumption, I crave
the cool hands of a friend, of a mother. When I return

the book to Aunt Ruby, handled with care, it is bone-clean,
unblemished; no blood, no sputum, no love.

Weighing our Breasts

When I dreamed I might be a dancer,
I disdained their encumbrance,
and much later, their pointless weight

that pulled at my shoulders, dragged down
towards a threat of widow's hump.
Where was the assurance

when we were young enough to want
the attention they could attract?
I just resented their bulk, though I might,

from time-to-time, knead them distractedly,
the way one might knead recalcitrant dough,
aware of their yielding substance, marvelling

at their inexplicable popularity, recalling
my grandmother stood in her garden,
arms crossed, hands cupped under her own

as if weighing them. Did she day-dream too —
of their early attraction, their practical
past, their uncertain future?

Pantomime

Now and then I remember Cinderella wandering backstage
bereft, wishing the transformation would last:

the pumpkin coach, the long-nosed rodent footman,
the incandescent wand that turns rags into

billowing tulle and sequin stars, Disney fashion.
Gossamer and squash are interchangeable

on stage. I think of our last meeting, how she
stood there with her prop-box gear, me half-

undressed in fishnet tights, gold boots, thigh-high;
how she said she forgot I wasn't her Prince

Charming, but someone old enough to be her mother,
wanted me to love her forever, carry her off

to my fairytale kingdom where the glass slipper always
fits; where the manager is not swinging her keys,

dying to get off before the pubs close, where the lame char
doesn't scowl, brandish her broom.

Portrait of my Daughter as a Portrait

The artist has chosen pastels
though I know her for her deeper shades,
for the heat of her fire: her reds, her oranges,
golds and yellows, the candour
of her turquoise.

Here, she is depicted in pinks and pastel blues,
a silk kimono draped loosely
over one shoulder.

I think I know every vertebra better; the arc
of shoulder, the point of elbow, its angle when bent,
the glimmer of her skin after dancing or bathing.

The artist has chosen white lilies for the table,
and I am astonished at this choice for my dahlia,
chrysanthemum, poppy daughter.

What can have happened between them to cause
this mutation: the white lampshade,
the lace table cover, the plush pink carpet
for my anything-in-turquoise daughter?

The way we know a daughter:
every dimple, every smile, every tantrum;
the way we do not.

Two Geckos

That gecko on the frieze above the door
is a designer gecko; the shape

of the head all wrong, an artsy gecko;
a tad pretentious, a figment

of some creative imagination; art deco gecko,
no relation to the ones we watched

at play each night around your doorway
by Rio Gordo, the fat dry river

absolutely still below us, or the one who
padded across the ceiling of the room

where I slept once; under the swallows' nest,
that you promised would not

crash down on me, showering nest, nestlings,
and bird shit over my blankets.

That painted gecko is the twin of the one
you had tattooed on your midriff years later

in Madrid, its slight form stretched below your high
tight breasts, your too-visible ribcage, the skin

barely disturbed; so accurate for what it was,
so perfectly placed on your adored body,

that I would never tell you how much I loathed
tattoos; how they brand you; mark you indelibly.

Surfeit

Take this field of feed corn, a buffet laid out
for red deer, muntjacs, or banquet
for vagrant squirrels.

Pheasants sashay down its aisles; guinea fowl,
their silver heads bobbing, weave in and out
between stalks that are Oklahoma high.

To our knees on moving day, we've watched it
in all its in-betweens — waist high when the books
were unpacked; just past our shoulders

when the paintings were hung — now towering
so far above our heads it shuts out the road,
the horizon, where the hills are spattered

with autumnal browns and golds. We stand in an aftermath
of empty cobs harvested by the creatures
who share this place, who warn

of shortages ahead — lean winter, uncertain spring. We gather
dead wood for our first fire, keep an uneasy eye
on the nettles, the fuel gauge, the headlines.

The Lisa Poems

i Uniform

The pinny is just about bearable;
the crackle of starch not unlike Father's distant
laughter — it's bound to get better soon,
we just need to hang on a bit longer.
She pulls the sash tight, proud of her tiny waist —
straightens the bow. The cap is more problematical;
its tiara of lace, ridiculous in the gilt mirror.
She tells herself one uniform is not unlike
another, but she remembers the limousine,
the chauffeur's peaked cap, the way he doffed it
when Mother got in, before the glass breaking.

ii The Good German

Beethoven, an Austrian, was dubbed 'The Good German' by Hitler

The way you might look at the gap where a clock
once hung in a former life, she looks back in time
as she watches the Proms on television, the tip
of her thumb nipped between front teeth

no longer her own, like a pensive child made solemn
by the puzzles of a grown-up world. I can see her face
from the door, intent in the Cathode flicker, her eyes
that barely blink at the antics of the first-row violinists:

their bows at pell-mell gallop; the strands of horse tails
that snap, catch the light like angel hair, the conductor
who stabs the air with his baton again and again.
She listens anew to Beethoven, whose deafness

might have earned him a place in the camps,
the showers; thrills to the entrance of the chorus
declaiming *Schiller, Freude schöner Götterfunken,*
Tochter aus Elysium, and the part of her

that was once a refugee bride, too poor for a seat,
when just being there was bliss, reaches out for the hand
of her man, the pair of them squeezing perfect joy
from late trains, the walk through drizzle or moonlight,

to tiny rooms at the other end of the world, or the tube line.
Locked in her own deafness she doesn't hear me,
sense me watching across generations.
I don't turn her head around to see.

iii Trike

The sticks were a slow capitulation
the backward progression from one to two

but the three-wheeler was an insult
which she hid in the garage

offered to visiting children for play
pretended she might one day

use it to shop   when she dreamed
the birthday trike

that whole summer by the lake   felt
her feet press the pedals

the way the wheels turned
slowly at first on grass or gravel

speeding up on earth then pavement
and before she knew it

she was streaming downhill in full sun
her plaits   their ribbons

her pinafore billowing out behind her   woke up
wondering what she ever did without it

left the sticks behind the door
to collect cobwebs dust time

iv Trolley

she's up again   hitting the trail
between her bed and the toilets
   escaped through a gap in the rails
         grabbed a trolley
her feet lodged in borrowed slippers

she doesn't believe the nurses
who tell her she's just been
   thumbs her nose
at their chart   its lying ticks

jaw set to stubborn
handles gripped tight
she might be heading for Cat Bells
   Striding Edge Helvellyn

she could be bound for freedom
but she'd settle for Milestone Wood
across the street and up the hill
from her house   past this year's daffs
   Budgens   the Indian Take-away

v Clearance

Table linen in neat piles, inset
with open-work lace and starched
stiff as sails in full wind,

and that it's raining

Sixty years of books, including
a fifties' *Encyclopaedia Britannica*,
German titles in *Alte Schrift*,

a letter from a relative in New York
offering affidavits to the family,
which saved some lives,

as the traffic outside gets heavier,
the tarmac dark with wet and swept
with the hiss of passing cars

and that it's still raining.

Family portraits of great-grandmothers —
both sides — coiffed, bombazined,
leg o' mutton sleeved; they glower

at this packing up, look set to protest
as the lamps that still have bulbs are lit
against the gloom inside,

the rain outside not letting up

the listing floor lamp,
the pair of matching Delfts,
their chipped bases,

the oval table, its fruitwood marquetry
defaced by the prints of careless drinkers;
you crying out, but refusing pain relief

and that it's raining, raining, raining.

vi Pegs

No one else wanted it,
its stout navy-blue cloth
drab and utilitarian.
Even the chain-stitched
letters embroidered
in not-quite-yellow,
meant to be gold, did not
raise interest. Only I
saw its usefulness at once;
how it served you on wash days,
how when you picked it up,
you'd remind us each time
the way your mother cooked
lentils on those days, always,
the smell of them cooking
as familiar to us as bleach
or starch; how with its long ties,
you could adjust it to the perfect
height –short for you, much
longer for me, and I could see
how it kept your hands free
for the many other tasks
you might encounter
on the way to the line
at the end of the scrubby lawn:
deadheading with your fingertips
or the secateurs you kept
nestled in its second pocket,
reaching out to caress the head
of a well-behaved child,
then freed up again
for shaking, stretching, tweaking
the sheets, the towels, your vests

so they hung as straight
on the sunlit line as your rows
of wallflowers, regimental daisies:
Ordnung müss sein.
Did you say it out loud
or have I made it up?

vii Turning her back

She turns her back to visitors —
not just ourselves, but all visitors:
her daughter, old friends, the rabbi,
a former carer, her last cleaner,
her grandchildren, one by one,
and last of all, my husband, her son.

She forces us to see how the house, chock full
of her past, kept her intact — how she fragments
in this room too full of light, air and strangers
who come and go in soft-soled shoes;
strangers who prod her into unwelcome
activity; who want to prop her up, spoon mush

between her reluctant lips, through some misguided
belief that she requires sustenance — when all she wants
is untroubled sleep, and we leave her — return
to our own sleep, troubled by the dream in which we arrive
again and again, to find her fully dressed, surrounded
by bags she has packed herself, smiling — ready for home.

viii The Viewing Suite

where they'd covered her nicely
a cozy red blanket
tucked in tight all around

we spoke in hushed tones
as if she could hear us as if
any moment

we'd see her breathing
that she'd speak

because she didn't look
that different
from when you'd seen her last

but when you placed your hand
on her forehead
smoothed her hair you said

she was cold

but the shock
was the blue tube
stuck in her mouth

a paramedic's crazed humanity

a last attempt
to keep her alive
despite her wishes

an insult to her last breath.

On a Road near Koronovo

after Vera Forster

Shots from behind, the guards prodding them
with the butts of their guns, how they tried
not to look at one another, dragged
their feet like sleepwalkers, along a road

lined with bystanders, the way a woman in a fur coat
reached out to turn her small daughter round,
buried the child's face against her, *for we were not,*
she says, *a sight for a child.* She remembers

when it began to snow, how Gerda in front slipped,
was not helped — the others would grab your coat
if you bent down to help — and once down,
you could not get up. And when she knew the march

could go on forever and ever, that the highway had no end,
there was a scuffle at the back, a stepping aside, and
a girl on a bicycle who must have ridden after them
all the way from the last town; the snow crunching

under her tyres, as slowly, cleverly, she swerved between
the staggering women, spoke to them in ice-puffs,
keep going, the Russians are catching up with you,
keep going, just ten kilometres, don't give up.

The women thought the guards would shoot her,
her flying coat an easy target, but in a breath her bicycle
veered off down a country lane and out of sight
as their army of ragged skeletons came to life,

began a dogged shuffle towards Koronovo. She cannot
recall the face of the girl, though she's tried
all her life, just the sound of her voice,
the snow, as it settled on her short fair hair.

Consider the Carousel

Consider the gilded lions, the jewelled horses,
the *Shtetl*, the wooden synagogues of Lithuania
where Marcus Illion, merry-go-round master,
taught his carvers their craft:
> painting and gilding foliage, fruits, animals,
to decorate the Torah arks, the horses exhausted
from their eternal gallop, tongues lolling,
nostrils flaring, dishevelled manes cascading,
ferocious red mouths.
> Consider the carousel at the end of the pier,
where the calliope wheezed and groaned;
where you rode, deafened, spinning, your arms
just too short to catch the brass ring. Scant hope
in this world where a mother could die in secret —
leave only the old and bereaved to guide her child,

still you hear yourself beg for another go.